INSTANT POT FOR TWO COOKBOOK

BY JEROME PATRICK

CONTENTS

CHAPTER 1: INSTANT POT OPTIONS & BASICS

One Pot – Multiple Benefits 6
Kills harmful micro-organism 6
Various Settings to Cook Various Cuisines 7
Special Instant Pot Functions 9
Instant Pot: Different Models For Different Needs 10

CHAPTER 2: BREAKFAST

Steel-Cut Oats with Dried Fruit 11
Easy-Peel Hard-Boiled Eggs 12
Banana Buckwheat Porridge 13
Berry Chia Oats 14
Instant Spiced Pilaf 15
Carrot Cake Oatmeal 16
Slow Cooked Ham and Egg Casserole 17
Wholesome Peach Oats 18

CHAPTER 3: BEANS & GRAINS

Superfood Quinoa Salad 19

Sausage Potato Rice Treat 20
Mango Rice Mania 22
Green Been Mushroom 23
Indian Style Instant Lentils 24

CHAPTER 4: FISH & SEAFOOD

Spicy Chili Snapper 26
Delicious Sesame Anchovies 28
Salmon Broccoli Meal.. 29
Wholesome Salmon Rice 30
Wisconsin Fish Boil 31
Foil-Steamed Tilapia 32
Swordfish Fra Diavolo 33
Spicy Mussels Mania 34

CHAPTER 5: MEATLESS MAINS

Quinoa Mixed Vegetable 35
Broccoli Chickpea.. 36
Walnut Been Lunch Bowl 37
Mushroom Wine Risotto 38
Instant Peas Risotto 40
Ginger Bean Potato... 41
Squash Mushroom Meal 42
Baked Ziti 43
Quick Mac & Cheese 44
Pasta Primavera.. 45
Mushroom Bean Farro 46
Spinach Pasta Treat.. 47

CHAPTER 6: CHICKEN

Classic Spiced Chicken Breats... 48
Honey Instant Chicken.. 50
Tender Cornish Hens with Gravy 51
Soothing Chicken Noodle Soup... 52

CHAPTER 6: BEEF & PORK

Ginger Pork Congee.. 53
Refreshing Wine Lamb Shanks 55
Spiced Beef Polenata 57
Hearty Beef Stew.. 58
American Chop Suey... 59

CHAPTER 7: SNACKS & APPETIZERS

Garlic Soy Tofu *60*
Bacon Cheese Muffins *61*
Tomato Eggpalnt Spread... *62*
Garlic Hummus *63*

CHAPTER 8: DESSERTS

Pumpkin Pie... *64*
Instant Fruit Bowl.. *65*
Fudgy Brownies *66*
New-York Cheesecake *67*
Orange Honey Yogurt Panna Cotta... *68*

Copyright 2017 - All rights reserved.

This document is geared towards providing exact and reliable information in regards to the topic and issue covered. The publication is sold on the idea that the publisher is not required to render an accounting, officially permitted, or otherwise, qualified services. If advice is necessary, legal or professional, a practiced individual in the profession should be ordered.

From a Declaration of Principles which was accepted and approved equally by a Committee of the American Bar Association and a Committee of Publishers and Associations.

In no way is it legal to reproduce, duplicate, or transmit any part of this document by either electronic means or in printed format. Recording of this publication is strictly prohibited, and any storage of this document is not allowed unless with written permission from the publisher. All rights reserved.

The information provided herein is stated to be truthful and consistent, in that any liability, regarding inattention or otherwise, by any usage or abuse of any policies, processes, or directions contained within is the solitary and utter responsibility of the recipient reader. Under no circumstances will any legal responsibility or blame be held against the publisher for any reparation, damages, or monetary loss due to the information herein, either directly or indirectly.

Respective authors own all copyrights not held by the publisher.

The information herein is offered for informational purposes solely and is universal as so. The presentation of the information is without the contract or any guarantee assurance.

The trademarks that are used are without any consent, and the publication of the trademark is without permission or backing by the trademark owner. All trademarks and brands within this book are for clarifying purposes only and are the owned by the owners themselves, not affiliated with this document.

CHAPTER 1: INSTANT POT OPTIONS & BASICS

Instant Pot is the modern version of a traditional stovetop pressure cooker. It is designed for automated cooking that demands less attention from its user. It comes with various cooking settings to make it an effortless cooking experience for you. All you need is to select the required cooking setting, add the recipe ingredients, close the lid and let instant pot cook delicious food for your whole family.

Its electric heating source generates high pressure inside to cook the added ingredients and can do all the functions that a slow cooker, rice cooker, steamer, and yogurt maker does.

One Pot – Multiple Benefits

Saves valuable time and energy

Instant Pot is designed for fast cooking and saves so much cooking time as compared to traditional cooking methods. Instant pot is insulated to prevent heat from escaping. By preventing heat escape, it saves energy needed to cook food. By cooking food in real quick time, it maintains your high energy level to carry out other important tasks.

Provides nutrient-rich food

As mentioned earlier, Instant Pot preserved essential nutrients of added ingredients by utilizing minimum liquid to cook food. Traditional cooking needs you to fully immerse the added ingredients underwater, while Instant Pot requires much less water and thus, prevents nutrients from being washed away.

Effortless cooking

Instant Pot provides you with flavorful cuisines in an effortless manner. It cooks food in an ideal method to make it tastier and healthier. It's simple to use with automatic cooking functions, and it is easy to clean also for a completely effortless cooking experience.

Kills harmful micro-organism

Instant Pot saves your body from many harmful bacteria and viruses by killing them in high-temperature cooking. Many cereals, vegetable, and pulses are prone to contain bacteria and fungus, even after washing them. Such bacteria and viruses get killed during the cooking process in Instant Pot.

Various Settings to Cook Various Cuisines

Rice
This is a special setting in which your Instant Pot transforms into a rice cooker. It cooks various rice varieties at low pressure and does the automatic cooking. You can use "Adjust" setting to increase or decrease cooking time.

Keep Warm/Cancel
In this setting, you can cancel any program that has been previously set. It is a useful cooking setting to put an Instant Pot in standby mode.

Bean/Chili
In this setting, you can cook different varieties of beans and chilies. The default with this setting is high pressure for 30 minutes.

Stew
In this setting, you can make all your favorite stew recipes. The default with this setting is high pressure for 35 minutes.

Soup
In this setting, you can make all your favorite soups and broth recipes. The default with this setting is high pressure for 30 minutes.

Porridge
In this setting, you can make all your favorite porridge and oatmeal recipes. The default with this setting is high pressure for 20 minutes.

Multigrain
In this setting, you can make all your favorite recipes from a mix of grains including different rice varieties, beans and so on. The default with this setting is high pressure for 40 minutes.
It comes with a 'MORE' setting with is set at 45 minutes of just warm water soaking for added grains. After soaking, instant pot cooks the soaked grains at high pressure for 2 hours. The 'LESS' setting is 20 minutes of cooking time.

Manual
In this setting, you can manually set your pressure and cook time.

Sauté
This setting is exclusively for open lid browning, sautéing, or simmering of common sautéing ingredients such as oil, onions, spices, garlic, veggies, etc.

Slow Cook
In this setting, Instant Pot slow cooks the added ingredients just like a slow cooker does. You can cook to up 40 hours. The default setting for the slow cook is 4 hours.

Steam
With this setting, you can steam veggies or reheating foods. The default with this setting is high pressure for 10 minutes.

Special Instant Pot Functions

NPR (Natural Pressure Release)
In this setting, you can naturally release pressure after your cooking time gets over. Leave the vent valve alone until it releases all inside pressure gradually. When you see the silver button on top of the lid go down, it means that all inside pressure has been released.

QPR (Quick Pressure Release)
In this setting, you can manually release the pressure in quick time as compared to natural release function. It is recommended to use a towel to cover the vent to diffuse anything that might come out because it involves a steady pressure of steam. Open the valve slowly to reduce the inside pressure.

PIP (Pot in Pot)
This is a special setting for adding another container inside Instant Pot. During pressure cooking, Instant Pot does not get as hot as an oven. Because of that, you need to cook by using stainless steel, silicone cups, glass, or any other oven proof container to place inside the pot.

Instant Pot: Different Models For Different Needs

Lux
Lux model is available in the market in two different sizes of 5 and 6 quart. This model has one disadvantage of not providing an option for low-pressure cooking. However, it can cook all the recipes with high-pressure setting. Lux model offers various pre-set temperature setting, and it has all the functions that a rice cooker/slow cooker has.

Duo
This model is available in the market in two different sizes of 6 and 8 quart. It is highly popular among instant pot users and lets you cook in both high pressure and low- pressure setting. This popular model offers various pre-set temperature setting and it has all the functions that a rice cooker/slow cooker has.

Smart
Smart model is a smart cooking device as the name suggests, it is designed to give you more control over your cooking techniques. It offers many customized settings for ease of cooking and effortless cooking experience.
This model comes with 11 pre-set temperature setting and lets you cook in both high pressure and low-pressure setting. It has all the functions that a rice cooker/slow cooker has. You can set delay timer for up to 24 hours. It has one special feature of cooking progress indicator.

CHAPTER 2: BREAKFAST

Steel-Cut Oats with Dried Fruit

Prep Time: 2 minutes

Cooking Time: 3 minutes

Number of Servings: 2

Ingredients:

- 1 cup steel cut oats
- 1 tablespoon butter
- 1 1/2 cups milk, plus more for serving
- 1 1/2 cups water
- 1 cup dried apricots or your favorite dried fruit

Directions:

1. Set the Instant Pot to Saute. Melt the butter in the bottom of the pan. 2. Add oats and toast until oats are lightly browned and smell nutty.
3. Pour in the milk, water, and dried fruit.
4. Close the lid and set cook time for 3 minutes on high pressure.
5. Ladle the oatmeal into pots and serve with milk.

Nutritional Values (Per Serving):
Calories - 435
Fat - 15.38 g
Carbohydrates - 80.59 g
Fiber - 12 g
Protein - 16.16 g

Easy-Peel Hard-Boiled Eggs

Prep Time: 1 minute

Cooking Time: 5 minutes

Number of Servings: 2

Ingredients:

    6 eggs
    1 cup water

Directions:

1. Pour the water into the pot. Place eggs in the steamer basket and set the basket over the water.
2. Close the lid and set the cook time for 5 minutes on high pressure.
3. After the pressure naturally releases, place the eggs in cold water.
4. Peel when cool enough to handle.

Nutritional Values (Per Serving):
Calories - 470
Fat - 13.22 g
Carbohydrates - 81.95 g
Fiber - 10.1 g
Protein - 13.04 g

Banana Buckwheat Porridge

Prep Time: 2 minutes

Cooking Time: 6 minutes

Number of Servings: 2

Ingredients:

- 1 cup buckwheat groats, rinsed
- 3 cups milk, plus more for serving
- 1 ripe banana, sliced
- 1 teaspoon ground cinnamon
- 2 tablespoons brown sugar, plus more for serving

Directions:

1. Pour the groats, milk, banana, cinnamon, and sugar into the Instant Pot.
2. Close the lid and set to 6 minutes on high pressure.
3. Serve porridge with additional milk and brown sugar.

Nutritional Values (Per Serving):
Calories - 409
Fat - 12.7 g
Carbohydrates - 62.26 g
Fiber - 4.5 g
Protein - 15.08 g

Berry Chia Oats

Prep Time: 5 min.

Cooking Time: 6 min.

Number of Servings: 2

Ingredients:

- 1/2 cups old fashioned oats
- 1/2 cups almond milk, unsweetened
- 1/2 cups blueberries
- 1 teaspoon chia seeds
- Sweetener or sugar as needed
- Splash of vanilla
- Pinch of salt
- A pinch ground cinnamon
- 1 ½ cups water

Directions:

1. In a medium bowl, thoroughly mix all the ingredients. Add the bowl mixture to a pint size jar and cover with an aluminum foil.
2. In the pot, slowly pour the water. Take the trivet and arrange inside it; place the jar over it.
3. Close the lid and lock. Ensure that you have sealed the valve to avoid leakage.
4. Press "Manual" mode and set timer for 6 minutes. It will take a few minutes for the pot to build inside pressure and start cooking.
5. After the timer reads zero, press "Cancel" and naturally release pressure. It takes about 8-10 minutes to release pressure naturally.
6. Carefully remove the lid and take out the jar. Mix in the oatmeal; serve warm!

Nutritional Values (Per Serving):
Calories – 114
Fat – 3g
Carbohydrates – 18g
Fiber – 4g
Protein – 4.5g

Instant Spiced Pilaf

Prep Time: 5-10 min.

Cooking Time: 5 min.

Number of Servings: 2

Ingredients:

1 stick cinnamon
1 cup millet, decorticated
2 pods cardamom
1 large onion, sliced
2 teaspoons whole cumin
1 ½ cups water
1 tablespoon oil
1 bay leaf
Salt as needed

Directions:

1. Take your Instant Pot and place it on a clean kitchen platform. Turn it on after plugging it into a power socket.
2. Put the pot on "Saute" mode. In the pot, add the oil and whole spices; cook until the cumin crackles.
3. Add the onions and cook for 2-3 minutes.
4. Turn off the pot and add the millet; cook for a few more minutes until the millet is well coated. Pour water and salt.
5. Close the lid and lock. Ensure that you have sealed the valve to avoid leakage.
6. Press "Manual" mode and set timer for 1 minutes. It will take a few minutes for the pot to build inside pressure and start cooking.
7. After the timer reads zero, press "Cancel" and naturally release pressure. It takes about 8-10 minutes to naturally release pressure.
8. Carefully remove the lid; fluff with the fork and serve warm!

Nutritional Values (Per Serving):
Calories – 315
Fat – 7g
Carbohydrates – 18.5g
Fiber – 0g
Protein – 3g

Carrot Cake Oatmeal

Prep Time: 10 minutes

Cooking Time: 10 minutes

Number of Servings: 2

Ingredients:

- 1 cup steel-cut oats
- 1 tablespoon butter
- 2 cups milk, plus more for serving
- 2 cups water
- 2 carrots, grated
- 1/4 cup brown sugar
- 1 teaspoon ground cinnamon
- 1/2 teaspoon nutmeg
- 1/2 cup raisins

Directions:

1. Set Instant Pot to Saute. Melt butter in the pot and add oats. Toast until oats are lightly browned and smell nutty.
2. Pour milk, water, carrots, sugar, cinnamon, nutmeg, and raisins into the pot.
3. Close lid and set cook time to 10 minutes on high pressure.
4. Serve with additional milk.

Nutritional Values (Per Serving):
Calories - 451
Fat - 17.4 g
Carbohydrates - 77.05 g
Fiber - 9.8 g
Protein - 16.57 g

Slow Cooked Ham and Egg Casserole

Prep Time: 10 minutes

Cooking Time: 1 hour 30 minutes

Number of Servings: 2

Ingredients:

- 6 eggs
- 1/2 cup plain Greek yogurt
- 1 cup shredded Cheddar cheese
- 1 cup ham, diced
- 1/4 cup fresh chives, chopped
- 1/2 teaspoon black pepper

Directions:

1. Whisk together eggs and yogurt. Stir in cheese, ham, chives, and pepper.
2. Pour the egg mixture into the Instant Pot.
3. Cover and set the cooking time for 90 minutes on the Slow Cook setting.
4. Slice into wedges and serve.

Nutritional Values (Per Serving):
Calories - 643
Fat - 43.44 g
Carbohydrates - 9.64 g
Fiber - 1.8 g
Protein - 51.27 g

Wholesome Peach Oats

Prep Time: 5 min.

Cooking Time: 10 min.

Number of Servings: 2

Ingredients:

- 2 medium size peaches, diced
- 1 cup oats
- 2 cups water
- 1 cup coconut milk

Directions:

1. Take your Instant Pot and place it on a clean kitchen platform. Turn it on after plugging it into a power socket.
2. Open the lid from the top and put it aside; start adding the mentioned ingredients inside. Thoroughly mix them.
3. Close the lid and lock. Ensure that you have sealed the valve to avoid leakage.
4. Press "Manual" mode and set timer for 10 minutes. It will take a few minutes for the pot to build inside pressure and start cooking.
5. After the timer reads zero, press "Cancel" and naturally release pressure. It takes about 8-10 minutes to naturally release pressure.
6. Carefully remove the lid. Sweeten as desired and serve warm!

Nutritional Values (Per Serving):
Calories – 189
Fat – 6.5g
Carbohydrates – 32g
Fiber – 9.5g
Protein – 15g

CHAPTER 3: BEANS & GRAINS

Superfood Quinoa Salad

Prep Time: 10 minutes

Cooking Time: 1 minute

Number of Servings: 2

Ingredients:

- 1 cup quinoa
- 1 cup water
- 2 tablespoons olive oil
- 2 tablespoons apple cider vinegar
- 1/2 teaspoon salt
- 1/2 teaspoon black pepper
- 1/2 avocado, diced
- 1 fresh tomato, diced
- 1/4 cup fresh cilantro, chopped

Directions:

1. Combine quinoa and water in a pot.
2. Close lid and set cooking time for 1 minute on high pressure.
3. While steam is releasing, make salad dressing. Whisk together oil, vinegar, salt, and pepper.
4. When quinoa is ready, toss with dressing, avocado, tomato, and cilantro. Serve warm or chilled.

Nutritional Values (Per Serving):
Calories - 529
Fat - 26.18 g
Carbohydrates - 61.91 g
Fiber - 10.3 g
Protein - 13.67 g

Sausage Potato Rice Treat

Prep Time: 5-8 min.

Cooking Time: 8-10 min.

Number of Servings: 2-3

Ingredients:
- 4 slices ginger
- 1 1/2 tablespoon green onion, finely chopped
- 3 cups water
- 1 teaspoon salt
- 2 cups long grain rice
- 1 tablespoon green onion, finely chopped
- 1/4 teaspoon chicken broth mix
- 1/6 teaspoon black pepper, ground
- 1 1/2 tablespoon olive oil
- 5 small yellow potatoes, peeled
- 2 lean sausages, thinly sliced

Directions:

1. Place your Instant Pot on a flat kitchen surface; plug it and turn it on.
2. To start making the recipe, press "Sauté" button. Add the oil, onions, and ginger; cook for 2 minutes to soften the ingredients.
3. Now add the sausages and cook for 1-2 minutes.
4. Add the potatoes and continue cooking for another 2 minutes. Then after, mix in the rice and stir to combine.
5. Add the remaining ingredients and carefully close its lid and firmly lock it. Then after, seal the valve too.
6. To start making the recipe, press "Rice" button. Now you have to set cooking time; set the timer for 4 minutes.
7. Allow the pot to cook the mixture until the timer goes off.
8. Turn off the pot and press "Cancel." Allow the built up pressure to vent out naturally; it will take 8-10 minutes to completely release inside pressure.
9. Open its lid and transfer the cooked mixture into serving container/containers.
10. Garnish with green onion and serve.

Nutritional Values (Per Serving):
Calories - 377
Fat – 12g
Carbohydrates – 55.6g
Fiber – 4g
Protein – 13.7g

Mango Rice Mania

Prep Time: 8-10 min.

Cooking Time: 5 min.

Number of Servings: 2-3

Ingredients:

    1 cup mango chunks
    2 tablespoon brown sugar
    1 cup white jasmine rice
    1 ¼ cup coconut milk, lightly sweetened
    1/3 cup coconut milk, lightly sweetened
    Black sesame seeds as needed

Directions:

1. Place your Instant Pot on a flat kitchen surface; plug it and turn it on.
2. Open the lid, and one by one add the rice, mango, and coconut milk (1 ¼ cup) in the pot. Carefully close its lid and firmly lock it. Then after, seal the valve too.
3. To start making the recipe, press "Manual" button. Now you have to set cooking time; set the timer for 4 minutes.
4. Allow the pot to cook the mixture until the timer goes off.
5. Turn off the pot and press "Cancel." Allow the built up pressure to vent out naturally; it will take 8-10 minutes to completely release inside pressure.
6. Open its lid and transfer the cooked mixture into serving container/containers.
7. Mix the coconut milk (1/3 cup) once done and mix well. Top with brown sugar alongside some sesame seeds. Serve warm!

Nutritional Values (Per Serving):
Calories - 261
Fat – 6g
Carbohydrates – 38.4g
Fiber – 3.2g
Protein – 4g

Green Been Mushroom

Prep Time: 5 min.

Cooking Time: 18-20 min.

Number of Servings: 2-3

Ingredients:

- 2 tablespoons butter
- 1 small onion, chopped
- 12-ounce sliced mushroom
- ½ cup green onions to garnish, chopped
- 16-ounce green beans
- 1 cup heavy cream
- 1 cup chicken broth

Directions:

1. Place your Instant Pot on a flat kitchen surface; plug it and turn it on.
2. To start making the recipe, press "Sauté" button. Add the oil, mushrooms, and onion; cook for 2-3 minutes to soften the ingredients.
3. Add the broth, beans and heavy cream. Carefully close its lid and firmly lock it. Then after, seal the valve too.
4. To start making the recipe, press "Manual" button. Now you have to set cooking time; set the timer for 15 minutes.
5. Allow the pot to cook the mixture until the timer goes off.
6. Turn off the pot and press "Cancel." Allow the built up pressure to vent out naturally; it will take 8-10 minutes to completely release inside pressure.
7. Open its lid and add 1-2 tablespoons of cornstarch to make it thicker.
8. Top with the green onions and serve.

Nutritional Values (Per Serving):
Calories - 353
Fat – 34g
Carbohydrates – 17g
Fiber – 3g
Protein – 9.4g

Indian Style Instant Lentils

Prep Time: 8-10 min.

Cooking Time: 45 min.

Number of Servings: 2-3

Ingredients:

- 1 teaspoon garam masala
- 2 tablespoons ghee or butter
- 3 cups water
- 2 tomatoes, chopped
- 1 teaspoon cayenne
- 1 bay leaf
- 1 large onion, chopped
- 1 tablespoon cumin seeds
- 1 teaspoon turmeric
- 1 1/2 inch ginger, minced
- 6 garlic cloves, minced
- 2 tablespoons avocado oil
- 1 cup whole and split lentils, soaked for 12-14 hours and drained
- 1/2 teaspoon black pepper
- Salt as needed
- Cilantro leaves (optional)

Directions:

1. Place your Instant Pot on a flat kitchen surface; plug it and turn it on.
2. To start making the recipe, press "Sauté" button. Add the oil and seeds; cook for 1 minutes; now add the onions and bay leaf; continue cooking for 8-10 minutes to soften the ingredients.
3. Add the spices, ginger, garlic, and combine well; add the tomatoes and sauté for 5 more minutes.
4. Add lentils and water and mix the ingredients; carefully close its lid and firmly lock it. Then after, seal the valve too.
5. To start making the recipe, press "Bean/chili" button. Now you have to set cooking time; set the timer for 30 minutes.
6. Allow the pot to cook the mixture until the timer goes off.
7. Turn off the pot and press "Cancel." Allow the built up pressure to vent out naturally; it will take 8-10 minutes to completely release inside pressure.
8. Open its lid and transfer the cooked mixture into serving container/containers. Add ghee, stir, then garnish with cilantro, and serve warm!

Nutritional Values (Per Serving):
Calories – 210
Fat – 14g
Carbohydrates – 15g
Fiber – 5.7g
Protein – 6.9g

CHAPTER 4: FISH & SEAFOOD

Spicy Chili Snapper

Prep Time: 20-25 min.

Cooking Time: 10-12 min.

Number of Servings: 2

Ingredients:

    2 teaspoons sugar
    1 red snapper, cleaned
    3 tablespoons chili paste
    1 tablespoon soy sauce
    1 green onion, chopped
    2 cups water
    1 garlic clove, minced
    ½ teaspoon ginger, grated
    2 teaspoons sesame seeds, toasted
    1 teaspoon sesame oil
    A pinch of sea salt

Directions:

1. Make some slits into the snapper and season with some salt and leave aside for 25-30 minutes.
2. Place your Instant Pot on a flat kitchen surface; plug it and turn it on.
3. Pour the water into the pot. Arrange the steamer basket in the pot and add the fish over the trivet.
4. Rub the snapper with the chili paste. Carefully close its lid and firmly lock it. Then after, seal the valve too.
5. To start making the recipe, press "Manual" button. Now you have to set cooking time; set the timer for 12 minutes.
6. Allow the pot to cook the mixture until the timer goes off.
7. Turn off the pot and press "Cancel." Allow the built up pressure to vent out naturally; it will take 8-10 minutes to completely release inside pressure.
8. Open its lid and transfer the cooked mixture into serving container/containers.
9. In a bowl of medium size, thoroughly mix the sugar with soy sauce, garlic, ginger, sesame seeds, sesame oil and green onion.
10. Serve the fish with the prepared sauce!

Nutritional Values (Per Serving):
Calories - 186
Fat – 12g
Carbohydrates – 23.5g
Fiber – 1g
Protein – 6.2g

Delicious Sesame Anchovies

Prep Time: 5 min.

Cooking Time: 4 min.

Number of Servings: 2

Ingredients:

- 1 tablespoon sesame seed oil
- ½ tablespoon vegetable oil
- 1 tablespoon sugar
- 1 cup anchovies, dried
- 2 garlic cloves, minced
- 1 tablespoon water
- Black sesame seeds to serve
- Roasted sesame seeds to serve

Directions:

1. In a bowl of medium size, thoroughly mix the water, garlic, and sugar; combine and set aside.
2. Place your Instant Pot on a flat kitchen surface; plug it and turn it on.
3. To start making the recipe, press "Sauté" button. Add the anchovies; cook for 1 minute.
4. Add vegetable oil, stir and cook for 1 minute more. Add the sugar mix. Carefully close its lid and firmly lock it. Then after, seal the valve too.
5. To start making the recipe, press "Manual" button. Now you have to set cooking time; set the timer for 2 minutes.
6. Allow the pot to cook the mixture until the timer goes off.
7. Turn off the pot and press "Cancel." Allow the built up pressure to vent out naturally; it will take 8-10 minutes to completely release inside pressure.
8. Open its lid and transfer the cooked mixture into serving container/containers. Add the sesame oil, black sesame seeds, and roasted seeds; stir and serve warm!

Nutritional Values (Per Serving):
Calories – 232
Fat – 17g
Carbohydrates – 7.4g
Fiber – 1.2g
Protein – 10.6g

Salmon Broccoli Meal

Prep Time: 8-10 min.

Cooking Time: 6 min.

Number of Servings: 2

Ingredients:

- 2 salmon fillets, skin on
- 1 cinnamon stick
- 1 tablespoon canola oil
- 1 cup water
- 2 cups broccoli florets
- 1 bay leaf
- 3 cloves
- 1 cup baby carrots
- pepper and salt as needed
- Some lime wedges for serving

Directions:

1. Place your Instant Pot on a flat kitchen surface; plug it and turn it on.
2. Open the lid, and one by one add the cinnamon, water, cloves, and bay leaf in the pot.
3. Add the steamer basket, add the salmon inside, season with salt and pepper and brush it with the oil.
4. Add the carrots and broccoli to the basket. Carefully close its lid and firmly lock it. Then after, seal the valve too.
5. To start making the recipe, press "Manual" button. Now you have to set cooking time; set the timer for 6 minutes.
6. Allow the pot to cook the mixture until the timer goes off.
7. Turn off the pot and press "Cancel." Allow the built up pressure to vent out naturally; it will take 8-10 minutes to completely release inside pressure.
8. Open its lid and transfer the cooked mixture into serving container/containers.
9. Serve warm with steamed carrots and broccoli, and fresh lime wedges.

Nutritional Values (Per Serving):
Calories – 421
Fat – 18g
Carbohydrates – 42.3g
Fiber – 16.2g
Protein – 32.4g

Wholesome Salmon Rice

Prep Time: 5 min.

Cooking Time: 5 min.

Number of Servings: 2

Ingredients:

- 1 cup chicken stock
- ½ teaspoon saffron
- ½ cup jasmine rice
- Salt and black pepper as needed
- 2 wild salmon fillets
- 1 tablespoon butter
- ½ cup veggie stock mix, dried

Directions:

1. Place your Instant Pot on a flat kitchen surface; plug it and turn it on.
2. Open the lid, and one by one add the stock, soup mix, rice, saffron, and butter in the pot.
3. Add the steamer basket in your pot, place salmon inside, season with salt and pepper. Carefully close its lid and firmly lock it. Then after, seal the valve too.
4. To start making the recipe, press "Manual" button. Now you have to set cooking time; set the timer for 5 minutes.
5. Allow the pot to cook the mixture until the timer goes off.
6. Turn off the pot and press "Cancel." Allow the built up pressure to vent out naturally; it will take 8-10 minutes to completely release inside pressure.
7. Open its lid and transfer the cooked mixture into serving container/containers.
8. Serve the salmon with rice on the side.

Nutritional Values (Per Serving):
Calories - 286
Fat – 12.4g
Carbohydrates – 18g
Fiber – 0.7g
Protein – 24.6g

Wisconsin Fish Boil

Prep Time: 10 minutes

Cooking Time: 9 minutes

Number of Servings: 2-3

Ingredients:

- 4 cups water
- 1 pound small red potatoes, halved
- 1 large onion, diced
- 2 carrots, sliced
- 2 stalks celery, sliced
- 1 lemon, halved
- 1 teaspoon salt
- 1/2 teaspoon pepper
- 2 pounds whitefish

Directions:

1. Place water, potatoes, carrots, onion, lemon, salt, and pepper into the Instant Pot.
2. Close the lid and set the cooking time for 7 minutes. Use quick release to remove the steam.
3. Add the whitefish to the pot. Close the lid and set the cooking time for 2 minutes.
4. Use quick release to remove the steam. Serve with buttered rolls.

Nutritional Values (Per Serving):
Calories - 405
Fat - 13.54 g
Carbohydrates - 23.29 g
Fiber - 2.9 g
Protein 46.08 g

Foil-Steamed Tilapia

Prep Time: 10 minutes

Cooking Time: 3 minutes

Number of Servings: 2

Ingredients:

- 4 tilapia fillets
- Juice of 1 lemon
- 1/2 tablespoon olive oil
- 1/2 teaspoon salt
- 1/2 teaspoon black pepper
- 4 garlic cloves
- 3 sprigs fresh dill

Directions:

1. Place the fillets on top of a sheet of aluminum foil. Season on both sides with lemon, olive oil, salt, and pepper. Place garlic and dill on top of the fish. Add another sheet of aluminum foil on top and fold in the edges to seal.
2. Pour 2 cups of water into the Instant Pot and add the foil package. Close the lid and set the cooking time for 3 minutes at high pressure.
3. Use quick release to remove the steam.

Nutritional Values (Per Serving):
Calories - 269
Fat - 7.46 g
Carbohydrates - 4.14 g
Fiber - 0.4 g
Protein - 47.14 g

Swordfish Fra Diavolo

Prep Time: 10 minutes

Cooking Time: 5 minutes

Number of Servings: 2

Ingredients:

- 2 tablespoons olive oil
- 4 garlic cloves, minced
- 1/2 teaspoon red pepper flakes
- 1 can whole peeled tomatoes, crushed
- 1/2 teaspoon salt
- 1/2 teaspoon black pepper
- 1 pound swordfish steaks

Directions:

1. Set the Instant Pot to Saute mode. Add garlic and red pepper flakes and cook until fragrant. Add tomatoes, salt, and pepper.
2. Place swordfish in the sauce. Flip once to coat.
3. Close lid and set cooking time to 3 minutes. After cooking time, use the quick release to remove steam. Serve with pasta.

Nutritional Values (Per Serving):
Calories - 427
Fat - 28.88 g
Carbohydrates - 5.81 g
Fiber - 2.1 g
Protein - 45.81 g

Spicy Mussels Mania

Prep Time: 5 min.

Cooking Time: 5 min.

Number of Servings: 2-3

Ingredients:

- 2 tablespoons olive oil
- 2 pounds mussels, scrubbed
- 1 yellow onion, chopped
- 14 ounces tomatoes, chopped
- ½ teaspoon red pepper flakes
- 2 teaspoons dried oregano
- 2 garlic cloves, minced
- ½ cup chicken stock

Directions:

1. Place your Instant Pot on a flat kitchen surface; plug it and turn it on.
2. To start making the recipe, press "Sauté" button. Add the pepper flakes, garlic, and onions; cook for 2-3 minutes to soften the ingredients.
3. Add the tomatoes, oregano, stock, and mussels; combine well. Carefully close its lid and firmly lock it. Then after, seal the valve too.
4. To start making the recipe, press "Manual" button. Now you have to set cooking time; set the timer for 2 minutes.
5. Allow the pot to cook the mixture until the timer goes off.
6. Turn off the pot and press "Cancel." Allow the built up pressure to vent out naturally; it will take 8-10 minutes to completely release inside pressure.
7. Open its lid and transfer the cooked mixture into serving container/containers.
8. Serve warm!

Nutritional Values (Per Serving):
Calories - 291
Fat – 10g
Carbohydrates – 11.2g
Fiber – 2g
Protein – 38.7g

CHAPTER 5: MEATLESS MAINS

Quinoa Mixed Vegetable

Prep Time: 5 min.

Cooking Time: 2 min.

Number of Servings: 2-3

Ingredients:

- 2 tablespoons soy sauce
- 2 tablespoons rice vinegar
- 1 thumb grated ginger
- 2 tablespoons of sugar
- 2 cups quinoa
- 4 cups water
- 8-ounce bag mixed vegetables, frozen

Directions:

1. Place your Instant Pot on a flat kitchen surface; plug it and turn it on.
2. Open the lid, and one by one add the mentioned ingredients in the pot except for veggies. Carefully close its lid and firmly lock it. Then after, seal the valve too.
3. To start making the recipe, press "Manual" button. Now you have to set cooking time; set the timer for 1 minute.
4. Allow the pot to cook the mixture until the timer goes off.
5. Turn off the pot and press "Cancel." Allow the built up pressure to vent out naturally; it will take 8-10 minutes to completely release inside pressure.
6. Open its lid and add in the vegetables; serve warm!

Nutritional Values (Per Serving):
Calories - 456
Fat – 7g
Carbohydrates – 42.3g
Fiber – 9.2g
Protein – 18g

Broccoli Chickpea

Prep Time: 8-10 min.

Cooking Time: 10 min.

Number of Servings: 2-3

Ingredients:

- 1/4 cup vegetable broth
- 1 (15 ounces) can chickpeas, drained
- Crushed red pepper as needed
- 3 large cloves of garlic, chopped
- 1 bunch broccoli rabe, halved
- Salt as needed
- 1/8 teaspoon fennel seeds
- 1/2 teaspoon olive oil

Directions:
1. Place your Instant Pot on a flat kitchen surface; plug it and turn it on.
2. To start making the recipe, press "Sauté" button. Add the oil and garlic; cook for 2 minutes to brown the garlic.
3. Add the seeds and red pepper; cook for 30 seconds. Then after, add the broccoli, broth, and chickpeas.
4. Carefully close its lid and firmly lock it. Then after, seal the valve too.
5. To start making the recipe, press "Manual" button. Now you have to set cooking time; set the timer for 4 minutes.
6. Allow the pot to cook the mixture until the timer goes off.
7. Turn off the pot and press "Cancel." Allow the built up pressure to vent out naturally; it will take 8-10 minutes to completely release inside pressure.
8. Open its lid and transfer the cooked mixture into serving container/containers.
9. Serve warm!

Nutritional Values (Per Serving):
Calories - 506
Fat – 10g
Carbohydrates – 44.3g
Fiber – 12g
Protein – 24.3g

Walnut Been Lunch Bowl

Prep Time: 5 min.

Cooking Time: 2 min.

Number of Servings: 2-3

Ingredients:

- 1 1/2 pounds beets, scrubbed, rinsed
- 2 cups water
- 2 teaspoons lemon juice
- 1 teaspoon Dijon mustard
- 2 teaspoons apple cider vinegar
- 1 1/2 tablespoons olive oil, extra virgin
- 2 tablespoons walnuts, chopped
- 1 1/2 teaspoons sugar
- Pepper and salt as needed

Directions:

1. Place your Instant Pot on a flat kitchen surface; plug it and turn it on.
2. Open the lid, and one by one add the water and beets in the pot. Carefully close its lid and firmly lock it. Then after, seal the valve too.
3. To start making the recipe, press "Manual" button. Now you have to set cooking time; set the timer for 10 minutes.
4. Allow the pot to cook the mixture until the timer goes off.
5. Turn off the pot and press "Cancel." Allow the built up pressure to vent out naturally; it will take 8-10 minutes to completely release inside pressure.
6. Open its lid and transfer the cooked mixture into a bowl.
7. Drain the beets and chop into bite-sized pieces.
8. In a mixing bowl; add all the ingredients for the dressing except oil and walnuts.
9. Whisk to combine thoroughly and add the olive oil slowly into the dressing; combine well.
10. Add the dressing over the beets, toss and serve!

Nutritional Values (Per Serving):
Calories – 151
Fat – 10g
Carbohydrates – 15.2g
Fiber – 3g
Protein – 2.7g

Mushroom Wine Risotto

Prep Time: 8-10 min.

Cooking Time: 10 min.

Number of Servings: 2-3

Ingredients:

- 2 teaspoons vegan butter
- 3 cups vegetable broth
- 2 cloves minced garlic
- 1 cup white onion, diced
- 1 1/2 cup Arborio rice, uncooked
- 1 teaspoon olive oil
- 1 ½ cups white mushrooms
- 1 ½ cups Portobello mushrooms, chopped
- ½ cup white wine
- 3 teaspoons lemon juice
- Ground pepper and salt as required

Directions:

1. Place your Instant Pot on a flat kitchen surface; plug it and turn it on.
2. To start making the recipe, press "Sauté" button. Add the butter (1 teaspoon) and both mushrooms; cook until the mushrooms turn soft. Set aside the mushrooms.
3. In the pot, add the oil, butter (1 teaspoon), garlic and onions; cook for 4-5 minutes to soften the ingredients.
4. Add the rice and combine well; cook to make the rice translucent. Then after, mix the wine, cooked mushrooms; cook until the wine evaporates.
5. Pour the stock and combine everything well. Carefully close its lid and firmly lock it. Then after, seal the valve too.
6. To start making the recipe, press "Manual" button. Now you have to set cooking time; set the timer for 5 minutes.
7. Allow the pot to cook the mixture until the timer goes off.
8. Turn off the pot and press "Cancel." Allow the built up pressure to vent out naturally; it will take 8-10 minutes to completely release inside pressure.
9. Open its lid and transfer the cooked mixture into serving container/containers.
10. Add the seasoning and lemon juice.
11. Serve warm!

Nutritional Values (Per Serving):
Calories – 339
Fat – 3g
Carbohydrates – 38.6g
Fiber – 1g
Protein – 6.3g

Instant Peas Risotto

Prep Time: 10 min.

Cooking Time: 10 min.

Number of Servings: 2

Ingredients:

- 1 cup baby green peas
- 1 cup Arborio rice
- 2 cloves garlic, diced
- 3 tablespoons olive oil
- 1 brown onion, diced
- ½ teaspoon salt
- 2 celery sticks, make small cubes
- ½ teaspoon pepper
- 2 tablespoons lemon juice
- 2 cups vegetable stock

Directions:

1. Take your Instant Pot and place it on a clean kitchen platform. Turn it on after plugging it into a power socket.
2. Put the pot on "Saute" mode. In the pot, add the oil, celery, onions, pepper, and salt; cook for 4-5 minutes until the ingredients become soft.
3. Mix in the zest, stock, garlic, peas, and rice. Stir the ingredients.
4. Close the lid and lock. Ensure that you have sealed the valve to avoid leakage.
5. Press "Manual" mode and set timer for 5 minutes. It will take a few minutes for the pot to build inside pressure and start cooking.
6. After the timer reads zero, press "Cancel" and quick release pressure.
7. Carefully remove the lid, add the lemon juice and serve warm!

Nutritional Values (Per Serving):
Calories - 362
Fat – 13g
Carbohydrates – 52.5g
Fiber – 3g
Protein – 8g

Ginger Bean Potato

Prep Time: 5 min.

Cooking Time: 10 min.

Number of Servings: 2-3

Ingredients:

- 1 teaspoon turmeric
- 1 large onion, chopped
- 1 cup garbanzo beans, cooked
- 1 cup diced tomatoes
- 2 potatoes, peeled & cubed
- 1/2 teaspoon salt
- 1/4 teaspoon ginger
- 1 teaspoon coriander
- 1/2 tablespoon whole cumin seeds

Directions:
1. Place your Instant Pot on a flat kitchen surface; plug it and turn it on.
2. To start making the recipe, press "Sauté" button. Add the 1/2 cup of water, cumin seeds, and onions; cook for 2-3 minutes to soften the ingredients.
3. Add the potatoes, turmeric, tomatoes, ginger, coriander, bean, salt and 1/4 cup water. Carefully close its lid and firmly lock it. Then after, seal the valve too.
4. To start making the recipe, press "Manual" button. Now you have to set cooking time; set the timer for 5 minutes.
5. Allow the pot to cook the mixture until the timer goes off.
6. Turn off the pot and press "Cancel." Allow the built up pressure to vent out naturally; it will take 8-10 minutes to completely release inside pressure.
7. Open its lid and transfer the cooked mixture into serving container/containers.
8. Serve the potatoes with your favorite bread or rice.

Nutritional Values (Per Serving):
Calories - 236
Fat – 2g
Carbohydrates – 42g
Fiber – 7.2g
Protein – 7g

Squash Mushroom Meal

Prep Time: 5-8 min.

Cooking Time: 15 min.

Number of Servings: 2

Ingredients:

- ½ cup almond slivers, toasted
- ¼ cup minced white onion
- 1 pound butternut squash, cubed
- 1 pound beans, sliced into 2-inch long slivers
- ⅛ cup minced chives
- 1 tablespoon olive oil
- 1 cup mushroom
- 1 cup vegetable broth, unsalted
- A pinch of white pepper
- ¼ teaspoon kosher salt

Directions:

1. Place your Instant Pot on a flat kitchen surface; plug it and turn it on.
2. To start making the recipe, press "Sauté" button. Add the oil and onions; cook for 4 minutes to soften the ingredients.
3. One by one add the mentioned ingredients in the pot (do not add the almonds, chives, and beans). Carefully close its lid and firmly lock it. Then after, seal the valve too.
4. To start making the recipe, press "Manual" button. Now you have to set cooking time; set the timer for 10 minutes.
5. Allow the pot to cook the mixture until the timer goes off.
6. Turn off the pot and press "Cancel." Allow the built up pressure to vent out naturally; it will take 8-10 minutes to completely release inside pressure.
7. Open its lid and add in the beans. Close lid and warm for 2 minutes to warm the beans. Adjust seasoning if needed.
8. Top with almond slivers and chives; serve warm!

Nutritional Values (Per Serving):
Calories – 406
Fat – 17g
Carbohydrates – 43g
Fiber – 18.3g
Protein – 28g

Baked Ziti

Prep Time: 10 minutes

Cooking Time: 10 minutes

Number of Servings: 2-3

Ingredients:

- 1 tablespoon olive oil
- 1 onion, chopped
- 2 cloves garlic, minced
- 2 cups whole peeled tomatoes with juice, crushed
- 1 pound uncooked ziti pasta
- 2 cups shredded mozzarella cheese

Directions:

1. Set the Instant Pot to Saute and add the olive oil, followed by the onion and garlic. Cook until onion is translucent.
2. Add tomatoes and pasta. Add enough water to cover the pasta and stir. Close the lid and set cooking time for 5 minutes at low pressure.
3. Use quick release to remove the steam, then open the lid. Arrange cheese over the pasta. Close the lid and allow to sit on Keep Warm setting 5 minutes or until cheese melts.

Nutritional Values (Per Serving):
Calories - 375
Fat - 17.11 g
Carbohydrates - 40.23 g
Fiber - 6.4 g
Protein - 16.83 g

Quick Mac & Cheese

Prep Time: 5 minutes

Cooking Time: 15 minutes

Number of Servings: 2-3

Ingredients:

- 1 pound uncooked macaroni
- 4 cups water
- 2 tablespoons butter
- 2 tablespoons flour
- 3 cups whole milk
- 1 cup shredded Cheddar cheese
- 1/2 teaspoon salt
- 1/2 teaspoon black pepper

Directions:

1. Combine the macaroni and water in the instant pot. Close the lid and set cooking time for 4 minutes on high pressure. After cooking time, use the quick release to remove the steam. Drain the pasta and wipe out the pot.
2. With pot set to Saute mode, melt butter. Add flour and cook until bubbling subsides and the mixture is slightly browned. Gradually add milk, stirring constantly, and cook until thickened slightly. Stir in cheese until melted. Season to taste with salt and pepper.
3. Stir in pasta. Heat through and serve.

Nutritional Values (Per Serving):
Calories - 713
Fat - 23.06 g
Carbohydrates - 97.02 g
Fiber - 3.8 g
Protein - 27.85 g

Pasta Primavera

Prep Time: 10 minutes

Cooking Time: 4 minutes

Number of Servings: 2-3

Ingredients:

- 1 pound penne pasta
- 4 cups water
- 2 zucchini, julienned
- 1 red bell pepper, julienned
- 1 onion, sliced thin
- 2 cloves garlic, minced
- 1 large tomato, diced
- 1/4 cup fresh basil, chopped
- 2 tablespoons olive oil
- 1/2 cup grated Parmesan
- 1/2 teaspoon salt
- 1/2 teaspoon black pepper

Directions:

1. Combine pasta and water in the Instant Pot. Place the steamer basket over the water and arrange zucchini, pepper, onion, garlic, and tomato in the basket. Close lid and set cooking time for 4 minutes on high pressure.
2. Use quick release to remove the steam. Drain the pasta. Pour the contents of the steamer basket into the pasta and toss with olive oil, basil, and Parmesan. Season to taste with salt and pepper.

Nutritional Values (Per Serving):
Calories - 283
Fat - 12.44 g
Carbohydrates - 33.15 g
Fiber - 3.9 g
Protein - 10.59 g

Mushroom Bean Farro

Prep Time: 8-10 min.

Cooking Time: 30 min.

Number of Servings: 2-3

Ingredients:

- 3 cups mushrooms, chopped
- 1 seeded jalapeno pepper, chopped
- 1 tablespoon shallot powder
- 2 tablespoons barley
- 1 tablespoon red curry paste
- ½ cup farro
- 1 cup navy beans, dried
- 2 tablespoons onion powder
- 9 garlic cloves, minced
- 2 tomatoes, diced
- Pepper and salt as needed

Directions:

1. Take your Instant Pot and place it on a clean kitchen platform. Turn it on after plugging it into a power socket.
2. Open the lid from the top and put it aside; start adding the beans, faro, barley, mushrooms, garlic, jalapeno, curry paste, shallot and onion powder, pepper and salt.
3. Add water to cover all the ingredients; gently stir them.
4. Close the lid and lock. Ensure that you have sealed the valve to avoid leakage.
5. Press "Manual" mode and set timer for 30 minutes. It will take a few minutes for the pot to build inside pressure and start cooking.
6. After the timer reads zero, press "Cancel" and naturally release pressure. It takes about 8-10 minutes to naturally release pressure.
7. Carefully remove the lid and add the tomatoes.
8. Sprinkle cilantro and scallions; serve warm!

Nutritional Values (Per Serving):
Calories - 238
Fat – 6.5g
Carbohydrates – 38g
Fiber – 1.5g
Protein – 11g

Spinach Pasta Treat

Prep Time: 5 min.

Cooking Time: 15 min.

Number of Servings: 2-3

Ingredients:

- 2 garlic cloves, crushed
- 2 garlic cloves, chopped
- 1 pound spinach
- 1 pound fusilli pasta
- A drizzle of olive oil
- ¼ cup pine nuts, chopped
- Black pepper and salt to taste

Directions:

1. Take your Instant Pot and place it on a clean kitchen platform. Turn it on after plugging it into a power socket.
2. Put the pot on "Saute" mode. In the pot, add the oil, garlic, and spinach; cook for 6-7 minutes until the ingredients become soft.
3. Add the pasta, salt, and pepper; add water to cover the pasta.
4. Close the lid and lock. Ensure that you have sealed the valve to avoid leakage.
5. Press "Manual" mode and set timer for 6 minutes. It will take a few minutes for the pot to build inside pressure and start cooking.
6. After the timer reads zero, press "Cancel" and quick release pressure.
7. Carefully remove the lid; mix the chopped garlic and pine nuts.
8. Serve warm!

Nutritional Values (Per Serving):
Calories - 198
Fat – 1g
Carbohydrates – 6.5g
Fiber – 1g
Protein – 7g

CHAPTER 6: CHICKEN

Classic Spiced Chicken Breats

Prep Time: 10 min.

Cooking Time: 15-20 min.

Number of Servings: 2-3

Ingredients:

- 1/8 teaspoon black pepper
- 1/8 teaspoon oregano, dried
- 1/8 teaspoon dried basil
- 3 chicken breasts, boneless and skinless
- 1/4 teaspoon garlic powder
- 1/2 teaspoon salt
- 1 tablespoon olive oil
- 1 cup water

Directions:

1. In a mixing bowl of medium size, combine the garlic powder, salt, black pepper, oregano, and basil. Rinse the chicken, pat dry and season one side with the ½ portion of the prepared mix.
2. Place your Instant Pot on a flat kitchen surface; plug it and turn it on.
3. To start making the recipe, press "Sauté" button. Add the oil and chicken, seasoned side down and then season the second side as well using remaining seasoning mix; cook for 3-4 minutes per side to soften the ingredients.
4. Then remove from the pot. Pour the water into the pot. Arrange the trivet in the pot and add the chicken over the trivet. Carefully close its lid and firmly lock it. Then after, seal the valve too.
5. To start making the recipe, press "Manual" button. Now you have to set cooking time; set the timer for 5 minutes.
6. Allow the pot to cook the mixture until the timer goes off.
7. Turn off the pot and press "Cancel." Allow the built up pressure to vent out naturally; it will take 8-10 minutes to completely release inside pressure.
8. Open its lid and transfer the cooked mixture into serving container/containers.
9. Serve warm!

Nutritional Values (Per Serving):
Calories – 324
Fat – 9.3g
Carbohydrates – 19.5g
Fiber – 2g
Protein – 42.3g

Honey Instant Chicken

Prep Time: 8-10 min.

Cooking Time: 25 min.

Number of Servings: 2-3

Ingredients:

- 1/2 teaspoon black pepper
- 1/4 cup ghee
- 2 pounds boneless chicken thighs, fresh or frozen
- 2 teaspoons garlic powder
- 1 1/2 teaspoons sea salt
- 1/4 cup honey
- 3 tablespoons tamari
- 3 tablespoons ketchup

Directions:

1. Place your instant pot on a flat kitchen surface; plug it and turn it on.
2. Open the lid, and one by one add the mentioned ingredients in the pot. Carefully close its lid and firmly lock it. Then after, seal the valve too.
3. To start making the recipe, press "Manual" button. Now you have to set cooking time; set the timer for 18 minutes for fresh chicken and 40 minutes if you are using frozen chicken.
4. Allow the pot to cook the mixture until the timer goes off.
5. Turn off the pot and press "Cancel." Allow the built up pressure to vent out naturally; it will take 8-10 minutes to completely release inside pressure.
6. Open its lid and transfer the cooked mixture into serving container/containers.
7. Serve warm with vegetables and rice.

Nutritional Values (Per Serving):
Calories – 544
Fat – 22g
Carbohydrates – 48.2g
Fiber –4g
Protein – 36.2g

Tender Cornish Hens with Gravy

Prep Time: 5 minutes

Cooking Time: 25 minutes

Number of Servings: 2

Ingredients:

- 2 small Cornish hens
- 1 teaspoon salt
- 1/2 teaspoon black pepper
- 1 teaspoon thyme
- 1/2 teaspoon rosemary
- 1 cup chicken stock
- 2 tablespoons flour
- 2 tablespoons water

Directions:

1. Rub the Cornish hens with salt, pepper, thyme, and rosemary. Place into Instant Pot and add the stock.
2. Close lid and set cooking time for 20 minutes. Use quick release to remove steam. Open the lid and transfer hen to a serving dish.
3. Set Instant Pot to Saute and bring the stock to a boil. Stir together flour and water in a small bowl. Pour into boiling stock, stirring constantly, and cook until thickened.
4. Serve gravy with the hen.

Nutritional Values (Per Serving):
Calories - 316
Fat - 8.34 g
Carbohydrates - 7.12 g
Fiber - 0.5 g
Protein - 49.6 g

Soothing Chicken Noodle Soup

Prep Time: 10 minutes

Cooking Time: 8minutes

Number of Servings: 2-3

Ingredients:

- 2 boneless chicken thighs, cubed
- 1 onion, diced
- 2 carrots, sliced
- 1 celery stalk, sliced
- 3 cups chicken stock
- 1/2 teaspoon salt
- 1/2 teaspoon black pepper
- 1 bay leaf
- 2 cups uncooked egg noodles

Directions:

1. Combine all ingredients in Instant Pot. Close lid and set cooking time for 8 minutes.
2. Discard bay leaf. Serve hot.

Nutritional Values (Per Serving):
Calories - 311
Fat - 17.31 g
Carbohydrates - 17.68 g
Fiber - 1.3 g
Protein - 20.21 g

CHAPTER 6: BEEF & PORK

Ginger Pork Congee

Prep Time: 5 min.

Cooking Time: 40-45 min.

Number of Servings: 2

Ingredients:

    3-century eggs, make small pieces
    2 thin slices ginger
    1 pound pork bones
    1 pound pork shank
    6 1/2 cups cold running tap water
    Salt as needed
    1 cup jasmine rice

Pork seasoning:
    A dash of ground white pepper
    1/4 teaspoon sesame oil
    1/2 teaspoon salt

Directions:

1. Place your Instant Pot on a flat kitchen surface; plug it and turn it on.
2. Open the lid, and one by one add the rice, pork, bones, ginger, and water in the pot. Carefully close its lid and firmly lock it. Then after, seal the valve too.
3. To start making the recipe, press "Manual" button. Now you have to set cooking time; set the timer for 35 minutes.
4. Allow the pot to cook the mixture until the timer goes off.
5. Turn off the pot and press "Cancel." Allow the built up pressure to vent out naturally; it will take 8-10 minutes to completely release inside pressure.
6. Open its lid and remove the bones and pork shank; shred the pork and season it with ground white pepper, 1/2-teaspoon salt, and 1/4 teaspoon sesame oil.
7. Add the eggs and stir well until you get the desired consistency.
8. Top with green onions and serve warm!

Nutritional Values (Per Serving):

Calories - 414
Fat – 18g
Carbohydrates – 15.2g
Fiber – 0.5g
Protein – 47.3g

Refreshing Wine Lamb Shanks

Prep Time: 10-15 min.

Cooking Time: 45 min.

Number of Servings: 2

Ingredients:

- ¼ cup olive oil
- 2 cinnamon sticks
- 1 medium onion, chopped
- 2 bay leaves
- 3 medium carrots, chopped
- 2 cups red wine
- 1 green chili pepper, sliced
- 3 lamb shanks
- 3 minced cloves garlic
- 1 tablespoon oregano
- 1 tablespoon smoked paprika
- 1 teaspoon cumin seeds
- 2 tablespoons water
- 2 teaspoons salt
- 2 tablespoons cornstarch
- 4 cups beef stock

Directions:

1. In a bowl of medium size, thoroughly mix the garlic, lamb, pepper, salt, paprika, oregano, cumin seeds, cinnamon sticks, and oil.
2. Coat well and place in a ziplock bag. Marinate for 4-6 hours.
3. Place your Instant Pot on a flat kitchen surface; plug it and turn it on.
4. To start making the recipe, press "Sauté" button. Add the oil (2 tablespoons) and lamb; cook to brown the lamb on both sides.
5. Add the leftover marinated mixture in the pot; add the carrots and onions, and cook to make them soft for 4-5 more minutes.
6. Add the wine and cook till the quantity reduces to its half. Add the stock and carefully close its lid and firmly lock it. Then after, seal the valve too.
7. To start making the recipe, press "Manual" button. Now you have to set cooking time; set the timer for 30 minutes.
8. Allow the pot to cook the mixture until the timer goes off.

9. Turn off the pot and press "Cancel." Allow the built up pressure to vent out naturally; it will take 8-10 minutes to completely release inside pressure.
10. Open its lid.
11. In another bowl, mix the water and cornstarch; combine it with the lamb mixture.
12. Simmer the mix in the pot to make it thicker.
13. Serve warm!

Nutritional Values (Per Serving):
Calories - 604
Fat – 44g
Carbohydrates – 12.5g
Fiber – 2g
Protein – 22.3g

Spiced Beef Polenata

Prep Time: 5 min.

Cooking Time: 8-10 min.

Number of Servings: 2

Ingredients:
- 1 tablespoon chili powder
- ¼ cup cilantro, chopped
- 2 teaspoons garlic, minced
- 1 bunch green onion, sliced
- 1 cup cornmeal
- 2 cups boiling water
- 2 cups vegetable broth
- ¼ teaspoon cayenne pepper
- 1 teaspoon oregano
- 1 teaspoon cumin
- ½ teaspoon smoked paprika
- Cooked beef meal of your choice

Directions:

1. Place your Instant Pot on a flat kitchen surface; plug it and turn it on.
2. To start making the recipe, press "Sauté" button. Add the oil, garlic, and onions; cook for 2-3 minutes to soften the ingredients.
3. Add the broth, cornmeal, spices, boiling water and cilantro and stir well. Carefully close its lid and firmly lock it. Then after, seal the valve too.
4. To start making the recipe, press "Manual" button. Now you have to set cooking time; set the timer for 5 minutes.
5. Allow the pot to cook the mixture until the timer goes off.
6. Turn off the pot and press "Cancel." Allow the built up pressure to vent out naturally; it will take 8-10 minutes to completely release inside pressure.
7. Open its lid and transfer the cooked mixture into serving container/containers.
8. Serve warm with your favorite beef meal!

Nutritional Values (Per Serving):
Calories – 136
Fat – 1.2g
Carbohydrates – 25.3g
Fiber – 1.6g
Protein – 3g

Hearty Beef Stew

Prep Time: 10 minutes

Cooking Time: 45 minutes

Number of Servings: 2

Ingredients:

- 1 pound chuck beef
- 1 teaspoon salt
- 1/2 teaspoon black pepper
- 2 tablespoons butter
- 1 onion, chopped
- 2 carrots, sliced
- 1 celery stalk, sliced
- 1 teaspoon thyme
- 1/2 teaspoon rosemary
- 2 tablespoons flour
- 1 tablespoon tomato paste
- 2 cups beef broth
- 1/2 pound potatoes, chopped

Directions:

1. Season the beef with salt and pepper. Melt the butter in the Instant Pot on Saute mode. Brown beef in butter. Remove to a plate.
2. Add onion, carrots, and celery to the pot. Cook until onion is translucent, then add thyme and rosemary and toast 30 seconds. Add flour and stir until everything is well-coated.
3. Add tomato paste, then beef broth and scrape off anything stuck to the bottom of the pot. Add potatoes and replace beef in pot.
4. Close lid and set cooking time to 35 minutes on high pressure. Season to taste with salt and pepper.

Nutritional Values (Per Serving):
Calories - 570
Fat - 25.33 g
Carbohydrates - 33.68 g
Fiber - 4.5 g
Protein - 53.64 g

American Chop Suey

Prep Time: 5 minutes

Cooking Time: 15 minutes

Number of Servings: 2-3

Ingredients:

- 1 tablespoon olive oil
- 1/2 pound ground beef
- 1 onion, diced
- 2 cloves garlic, minced
- 1 can whole tomatoes in their juice, crushed
- 1/2 cup beef stock
- 1 tablespoon Worcestershire sauce
- 1/2 teaspoon salt
- 1/2 teaspoon black pepper
- 1/2 pound uncooked macaroni
- 1 cup shredded mozzarella cheese

Directions:

1. Heat olive oil in Instant Pot on Saute mode. Brown beef and drain excess fat, then add onions and garlic.
2. Pour in tomatoes, stock, Worcestershire, salt, and pepper. Stir in pasta and half of the cheese.
3. Close lid and set cooking time to 8 minutes on high pressure. Use quick release to remove steam.
4. Sprinkle the remaining cheese over the pasta and close lid until the cheese is melted. Serve.

Nutritional Values (Per Serving):
Calories - 495
Fat - 19.89 g
Carbohydrates - 48.74 g
Fiber - 3.3 g
Protein - 29.07 g

CHAPTER 7: SNACKS & APPETIZERS

Garlic Soy Tofu

Prep Time: 5 min.

Cooking Time: 2 ½ hours

Number of Servings: 2

Ingredients:

- 1/2 tablespoon apple cider vinegar
- 1 tablespoon soy sauce
- 1 container extra firm tofu, cut to make 1-inch cubes
- 1/4 teaspoon garlic powder
- 1/2 tablespoon red pepper flakes
- 3/4 cup ketchup
- 1/4 teaspoon salt
- 1 1/2 tablespoon brown sugar

Directions:

1. Place your Instant Pot on a flat kitchen surface; plug it and turn it on.
2. Open the lid, and one by one add the mentioned ingredients in the pot. Stir to combine well.
3. Carefully close its lid and firmly lock it. Then after, seal the valve too.
4. To start making the recipe, press "Slow Cook" button. Now you have to set cooking time; set the timer for 2 hours 30 minutes.
5. Allow the pot to cook the mixture until the timer goes off.
6. Turn off the pot and press "Cancel". Allow the built up pressure to vent out naturally; it will take 8-10 minutes to completely release inside pressure.
7. Open its lid and transfer the cooked mixture into serving container/containers.
8. Serve warm!

Nutritional Values (Per Serving):
Calories – 433
Fat – 5.3g
Carbohydrates – 27.2g
Fiber – 4g
Protein – 15g

Bacon Cheese Muffins

Prep Time: 8-10 min.

Cooking Time: 8-10 min.

Number of Servings: 2-3

Ingredients:

    4 tablespoons cheddar cheese, shredded
    ¼ teaspoon lemon pepper seasoning
    4 slices precooked bacon, crumbled
    1 green onion, diced
    4 eggs

Directions:

1. Place your Instant Pot on a flat kitchen surface; plug it and turn it on.
2. Arrange a steamer basket inside the pot and add 1 1/2 cups of water.
3. In a bowl, break 4 eggs and whisk well. Add the lemon pepper and beat everything well.
4. Divide the green onion, bacon, and cheese into 4 muffin cups. Top with the egg mixture and stir to combine well.
5. Arrange the cups on the steamer basket, cover it and then lock the lid.
6. To start making the recipe, press "Manual" button. Now you have to set cooking time; set the timer for 8 minutes.
7. Turn off the pot and press "Cancel." Quick release inside pressure.
8. Serve warm!

Nutritional Values (Per Serving):
Calories - 170
Fat – 13g
Carbohydrates – 1g
Fiber – 0g
Protein – 12g

Tomato Eggpalnt Spread

Prep Time: 5-8 min.

Cooking Time: 10 min.

Number of Servings: 2-3

Ingredients:

- 3 tablespoons olive oil
- 1 cup yellow onion, chopped
- 2 minced garlic cloves
- 2 cups eggplant, chopped
- 1 cup sweet bell pepper, chopped
- ¼ cup sun-dried tomatoes, minced
- 2 tablespoons tomato paste
- ¼ cup vegetable stock
- Black pepper and salt as needed

Directions:
1. Take your Instant Pot and place it on a clean kitchen platform. Turn it on after plugging it into a power socket.
2. Put the pot on "Saute" mode. In the pot, add the oil and onion; cook for 2-3 minutes until the ingredients become soft.
3. Mix in the garlic, bell pepper, and eggplant; stir and cook for 2 minutes more.
4. Add the tomatoes, stock, salt, pepper and tomato paste; stir gently.
5. Close the lid and lock. Ensure that you have sealed the valve to avoid leakage.
6. Press "Manual" mode and set timer for 5 minutes. It will take a few minutes for the pot to build inside pressure and start cooking.
7. After the timer reads zero, press "Cancel" and quick release pressure.
8. Carefully remove the lid. Serve on toasted bread as an appetizer.

Nutritional Values (Per Serving):
Calories - 162
Fat – 4g
Carbohydrates – 7.5g
Fiber – 3g
Protein – 8g

Garlic Hummus

Prep Time: 10 minutes

Cooking Time: 35 minutes

Number of Servings: 2

Ingredients:

- 1 cup dry chickpeas
- 2 cups water
- 1/2 cup tahini
- 3 garlic cloves, minced
- Juice of 1 lemon
- 1/4 teaspoon cumin
- 1/2 teaspoon salt
- 1/2 teaspoon black pepper

Directions:

1. Place chickpeas in Instant Pot with water. Close lid and set cooking time to 35 minutes on high pressure.
2. When steam is removed, drain beans and transfer to a food processor or blender. Add tahini, garlic, lemon, cumin, salt, and pepper. Blend until smooth. Season to taste with additional salt, pepper, and lemon.
3. Serve with pita bread or chips.

Nutritional Values (Per Serving):
Calories - 375
Fat - 19.23 g
Carbohydrates - 39.7 g
Fiber - 9.1 g
Protein - 15.58 g

CHAPTER 8: DESSERTS

Pumpkin Pie

Prep Time: 10 minutes

Cooking Time: 35 minutes

Number of Servings: 2-3

Ingredients:

    1 prepared graham cracker pie crust in aluminum pan
    1 can pumpkin
    1/2 cup milk
    1 egg
    1/2 cup brown sugar
    1 teaspoon cinnamon
    1/2 teaspoon nutmeg

Directions:

1. Blend together pumpkin, milk, egg, sugar, cinnamon, and nutmeg. Pour into prepared graham cracker crust.
2. Place the trivet in the pot and pour in enough water to reach just the top of the trivet. Place the pie over the trivet.
3. Close the lid and set cooking time for 35 minutes on high pressure. Chill pie before serving.

Nutritional Values (Per Serving):
Calories - 413
Fat - 13.85 g
Carbohydrates - 68.5 g
Fiber - 4.8 g
Protein - 6.1 g

Instant Fruit Bowl

Prep Time: 8-10 min.

Cooking Time: 10 min.

Number of Servings: 2

Ingredients:

- 1 apple, chopped
- 2 tablespoons granular stevia or sugar
- 1 plum, chopped
- 1 pear, chopped
- ½ teaspoon cinnamon
- 3 tablespoons coconut oil
- 1 cup water
- ¼ cup coconut, shredded
- ¼ cup pecans, chopped

Directions:

1. In a bowl (heatproof) of medium size, thoroughly mix the plum, apple, pear, coconut oil, coconut, cinnamon and stevia/sugar.
2. Take your instant pot and place it on a clean kitchen platform. Turn it on after plugging it into a power socket.
3. In the pot, slowly pour the water. Take the trivet and arrange inside it; place the bowl over it.
4. Close the lid and lock. Ensure that you have sealed the valve to avoid leakage.
5. Press "Manual" mode and set timer for 10 minutes. It will take a few minutes for the pot to build inside pressure and start cooking.
6. After the timer reads zero, press "Cancel" and quick release pressure.
7. Carefully remove the lid; divide into bowls and serve with pecans on top.

Nutritional Values (Per Serving):
Calories - 150
Fat – 4g
Carbohydrates – 13.5g
Fiber – 4g
Protein – 6.5g

Fudgy Brownies

Prep Time: 10 minutes

Cooking Time: 20 minutes

Number of Servings: 2-3

Ingredients:

- 1/2 cup butter
- 1 cup sugar
- 2 eggs
- 1 teaspoon vanilla
- 2/3 cup flour
- 1/3 cup cocoa powder
- 1/2 teaspoon baking powder
- 1/2 teaspoon salt

Directions:

1. Cream butter and sugar, then beat in eggs one at a time. Add vanilla last. In a separate bowl, whisk together flour, cocoa, baking powder, and salt. Fold dry ingredients into wet ingredients. Pour batter into a baking pan that fits into the Instant Pot.
2. Place a trivet in the Instant Pot. Add enough water to just reach the top of the trivet. Place the baking pan over the trivet.
3. Close the lid and set the cooking time to 20 minutes. Serve brownies warm or room temperature.

Nutritional Values (Per Serving):
Calories - 524
Fat - 26.25 g
Carbohydrates - 70.72 g
Fiber - 2.7 g
Protein - 6.45 g

New-York Cheesecake

Prep Time: 10 minutes

Cooking Time: 25 minutes

Number of Servings: 2-3

Ingredients:

- 1 prepared graham cracker crust in aluminum pan
- 1 package cream cheese, softened
- 1/2 cup sour cream
- 2 eggs
- 2/3 cup sugar
- 2 tablespoons cornstarch
- 2 teaspoons vanilla

Directions:

1. Beat together cream cheese, sour cream, eggs, sugar, cornstarch, and vanilla. Pour into pie crust.
2. Place a trivet in the Instant Pot. Add enough water to reach the top of the trivet. Place the pie pan on the trivet.
3. Close lid and set cooking time for 25 minutes on high pressure. Chill before serving.

Nutritional Values (Per Serving):
Calories - 523
Fat - 23.78 g
Carbohydrates - 69.89 g
Fiber - 0.9 g
Protein - 7.37 g

Orange Honey Yogurt Panna Cotta

Prep Time: 25 minutes

Cooking Time: 1 minute

Number of Servings: 2

Ingredients:

- 1 cup Basic Yogurt (recipe above)
- 1/4 cup sugar
- 1 teaspoon vanilla
- 1 tablespoon hot water
- 1 teaspoon unflavored gelatin
- 1/4 cup honey
- Juice of 1 orange with pulp
- 1/4 teaspoon cardamom

Directions:

1. Whisk together yogurt, sugar, and vanilla.
2. Sprinkle gelatin over water and allow to soften. Whisk together until gelatin dissolves. Whisk gelatin mixture into yogurt mixture.
3. Pour yogurt mixture into two small ramekins or one large ramekin. Chill 2 hours.
4. Meanwhile, make a sauce. Combine honey, orange, and cardamom in the Instant Pot. Close lid and set cooking time to 1 minute. Chill completely.
5. When panna cotta is set, run a knife around the inside of the ramekin and invert onto a plate. Top with sauce.

Nutritional Values (Per Serving):
Calories - 343
Fat - 4.1 g
Carbohydrates - 75.25 g
Fiber - 1.7 g
Protein - 5.08 g

Thank you for buying this book!

I hope this book was able to help you.

Made in the USA
Middletown, DE
08 March 2018